Church Girl

My Search for Acceptance

By

Anita M. Hoover

Illustrated by
Emmanuel Hoover

ISBN: 1-4107-5260-7 (e-book)
ISBN: 1-4107-5261-5 (Paperback)

This book is printed on acid free paper.

1stBooks – rev. 12/01/03

"DON'T BLAME THE PASTOR..."

What you are about to read is a true story.
The names and events are real.
Don't be surprised if what you read sounds like someone you know. It's possible.
There's at *least* one "Church Girl" in *every* church.
But guess what,
IT"S NOT NECESSARILY THE PASTOR'S FAULT!

The events that took place in my life were MY CHOICES. Not a lack of teaching. Not a lack of "Youth programs".
Sometimes we accuse Pastors of being negligent, or "not spiritual" when we hear of their members "cutting up".

Unless _God_ chooses to _reveal_ what's going on in someone's life to a Pastor, it is not his job to keep us under 24-hour surveillance- that's what the Holy Ghost is for!

If by chance you _feel_ you are at a church where the Pastor is not preaching and teaching like he should, PRAY.
If you _know_ you're at a church where the Pastor is not preaching and teaching like he should, PRAY...and allow the LORD to lead you to one that is.

God said HE would give us Pastors according to HIS heart;

Shepherds, to feed us with knowledge and understanding.
My Pastor was chosen by God to Pastor me. He did his job.

Because of his consistency, preaching the Gospel of Jesus Christ, and teaching true repentance and true holiness,
I had everything I needed to make my decision.

<u>CHOICES</u> WILL ALWAYS BE OURS!

Table of Contents

"MY SEARCH FOR ACCEPTANCE"

My past. Better known as my search for ACCEPTANCE. Like most young people, I wanted very much to "enjoy life" like my "friends". I wanted to dance and date like "everybody else my age"; but my saved, sanctified and filled with the Holy Ghost Mom wouldn't stand for that. I tried really hard at first to do it "her way" because I had been told what the Bible said about obedience to parents; but I got tired of being laughed at and left out. So how did I "solve" the problem?

Well, I'd decided early in grammar school that drugs weren't for me. To me it was too risky. I mean what if someone gave me some "bad" stuff?

I WAS SCARED!

Instead, I solved that "problem" by just hanging out with my "friend", whom by the way, wasn't scared of anything. It wasn't long before he and a few other "friends" showed me how to dance, date and do drugs...behind my saved, sanctified, filled with the Holy Ghost Mom's back.

I was able to dodge Mom's watchful eye until my sophomore year in high school. I got pregnant and dropped out. My "friend" / baby's father left. He went to college. I only saw him twice after that. After my baby came, my parents helped me get a GED. Shortly after, I found a job and started working full time during the day while taking computer classes at night.

Things went well for awhile. I was making money and furthering my education. Hey, that's what life is all about, right? YEAH, SURE!

Busy as I was , there still didn't seem to be enough "life" in my life, so I decided to get more active in church. Well, *sincere* as I was about "church", I still couldn't bring myself to let go of my main hindrance aka "friends" – new BOYfriend in particular. Oh, he didn't mind me going to church, singing in the choir, helping out with little kids and Sunday School. He even found himself a Bible and came to church with me. What he *did* mind was *not* having sex! Yep, I was back on that mission again trying to hold out. But I needed something greater than a promise to myself. I needed the power of God!

I tried to explain to him what the Bible says about sex outside of marriage

"Marriage is honorable in all and the bed undefiled, but whoremongers and adulterers God will judge".

Hebrews 13:4 KJV

That went in one ear and out of the other. In almost no time I found myself "engaged". The next thing I knew, I found myself "shacking up". Now I *knew* deep inside it was wrong, but he would "change" after we got married, right? YEAH, SURE! We never got married; he never changed, but I did.

He began to "blame" the church for coming between us because there were still many things I didn't want to do that he enjoyed.

In fact, it wasn't long before he stopped going to church altogether. Somehow I came to the conclusion that maybe if I did *some* of the stuff he liked *and* kept going to church he wouldn't see me as being "self-righteous". I was hoping I could pray our relationship into something successful.

Well, like I said he never changed; eventually I had to face the fact that

God was not honoring my prayers for "us" – because *I didn't qualify to pray for "us"* - because *I was knowingly and willfully living in SIN* . Instead of the relationship getting better, it got worse. He lost his job and began drinking. He was also heavily involved with drugs.

He stole from me to support his habit, sometimes not even leaving me enough money to get to work and certainly not to keep up with my tuition. Eventually I lost my job too, and had to drop out of school without finishing (again). It wasn't long before I found myself drinking, and using drugs right along with him!

Besides the reefers, I had no idea what else I was smoking. I just knew it was NOT a cigarette and it was NOT legal. *I did not enjoy getting high*, it just seemed to be the only way I could get my mind off my problems. But of course the high didn't last and the high also cost money, which was something neither of us had to spare.

Thank God! Not having the money to support my "little" habit probably helped me stop before becoming an addict. Speaking of money, let me tell you about a certain rich man Jesus spoke of in the gospel according to Luke 12:16 – 21.

There was a certain rich man who was very prosperous. The Bible says his grounds brought forth *plentifully.* He began to think to himself, "Hmm. Let's see. I've made all this money, own all this property...what am I going to do with all this stuff I've gained?"

He thought a bit longer and came up with what he thought was the perfect solution.

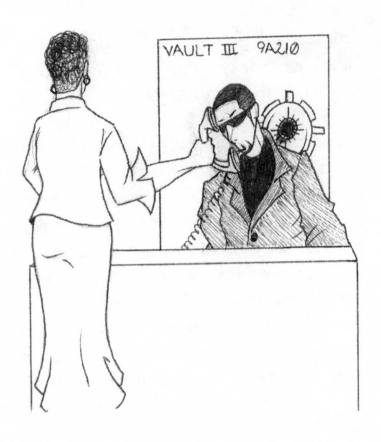

He decided, "I'll build new storehouses to keep all my stuff. As a matter of fact, I think I'll throw myself a little ground-breaking party to celebrate; after all I have plenty of money saved up...I'm going to relax, eat, drink and be merry!"

Sounds pretty cool, right? Just chill with some food, folks and fun right? YEAH ,SURE! As he sat with his chest puffed out, patting himself on the back for all of his major accomplishments, trying to decide what move to make next, his plans were suddenly INTERRUPTED!!!

The Bible says the Lord spoke to the rich man and said,

"You fool! Tonight your soul will be required of you"! His life was about to end suddenly; he was about to lose his soul and he didn't even know it!

So many of us young people think just like this rich man. We often feel that all we need is money. For those of us that feel money is not a problem – something else may be. Apparently for this rich man, money was the main problem – or rather his attitude toward money.

He felt that he could just do whatever he wanted, (eat, drink, be merry) because he had the money to pay for it. He thought he was in complete control of everything around him. But as rich as he was, he was unable to buy another day of *life!*

Most of us have been taught to go after whatever will make us the best off financially. Attractive men and women are encouraged to become models and go into movies; the musically talented often dream of going platinum. Every writer wants to be credited with the bestseller, and no matter one's talent (or lack of), everyone is in favor of getting the best education.

Well, there is nothing wrong with any of these pursuits, however it's important to keep in mind that while the best looks, the best voice, the best car, the best "connections" and yes, the best education, can take you places, any of these things can become a false god to you and take you to HELL! One of the church mothers put it best...

"You need Jesus on your mind!
Get Jesus on your mind!
You can go to college,
You can go to school,
But if you ain't got JESUS...
You're just an EDUCATED FOOL!Get Jesus, get Jesus on your mind!"

Now, the closest thing, or rather person to many people is their mother.

For others it may be a boyfriend, girlfriend, even a husband or wife.

In Matthew 10:37 Jesus used one of the closest examples of relationships that should not take priority over your relationship with Him. He said:

"He [or she] that loveth father or mother more than Me is not worthy of Me"

If the Lord doesn't want your relationship with your parents to come between you and Him, how do you think He feels about your "relationship" with the things you possess? The rich man Jesus spoke of had it all together – a financial genius I'm sure his friends thought. But what did the *Lord* think about this "genius"?

The *Lord* called him a FOOL!

Mind you that regardless of how we may have impressed our friends, if we think like this rich man, the *Lord* holds the same opinion of us as He did the rich man.

"So is he (a fool) that layeth up treasure for himself and is not rich toward God." Luke 12:21

Am I suggesting we all drop out of school , quit our jobs and become full time Sunday school students and preachers? NO!

I'm praying like John in the Bible :

"....that you would prosper and be in health even as your SOUL prospers".

3 John:2

IT'S ABOUT BALANCE!

It's about being able to use our God-given gifts to sustain ourselves financially (Deuteronomy 8:18), to meet the needs of others (1 Corinthians 12) and ultimately bring glory to GOD (1 Corinthians 3:21-23), who is the Giver of EVERY good and perfect gift (James 2:17)! What have you stored up for yourself? Check *your* "BALANCE"!

Now, as I was saying, my boyfriend's "peddling" and my monthly check from public aid didn't amount to very much money between us. But hey, money isn't everything right? I mean, at least we had each other, right?

YEAH, SURE! That's what I thought until one night my boyfriend got a little "too high". He tried to kill me.

His sister arrived just in time to witness him swing a baseball bat to my head. I was standing next to one of the wood beams dividing the living and dining rooms , but he swung too fast for me to think about ducking – there was a loud "CRACK". I opened my eyes and on the floor was *half* a bat and large slivers of wood from the beam. MIRACULOUSLY, he missed *me!*

As he came at me again, his sister's boyfriend tried to sneak up and grab him from behind; I remember her screaming at me "Run...he's going to kill you...!" I heard and didn't hear. I stood frozen in total shock. By the time I snapped out of it, it was too late...

The next morning, two police officers escorted me from the hospital back to the apartment to gather my few remaining belongings...one sweater and a coat. I'll never forget what one of the officers said to me that day:

"I don't know why beautiful girls like you keep settling for guys like him. You're not even his type. You look like you should be in church somewhere, singing in somebody's choir".

Sounds like an old pick-up line doesn't it? But he was telling the truth and it cut me like I knife. Church was all I had ever known. So how was I drawn so far away? How did I ever think I could get away with doing the things I knew were wrong? Why did I even try?

The answer for me was FEAR!

FEAR of spending my whole life in church without ever experiencing anything else.

FEAR of always being laughed at and left out.

FEAR of never being good enough at anything to be as successful as someone else (because I had not graduated from school like "everyone" else).

FEAR of growing old...ALONE.

Now, you're probably wondering how someone who spent their entire life in church hearing about the love of God and power of Jesus Christ could feel so *un*loved and afraid. Here's how.

Sunday after Sunday, thousands of churches are packed with people who attend and even enjoy a church "service", perhaps the same way you or some of your friends have gone to the show, or even attended school. Someone is there to show and tell you something. They're able to hold your attention, even make you laugh. But do you go home a *changed person*? Maybe. Maybe not

On the other hand you may be like some unfortunate young people who managed to drift through school and even walk across the "stage" with the rest of the graduating class, but time tells if you *really* learned anything; if you really did your "homework'! Well, for me church was exciting and fun. But when it came to living for God the rest of the week, I had a long list of "missing assignments!"

Okay. I'll give you the benefit of the doubt. You're not lazy like I was. You try your best to pay attention, to do all your work, but for some reason you just can't seem to catch on. Well, that's why there's a thing called TUTORING. Someone who knows what to do (AND how to explain it) sits down with you one on one and walks you through the process until you get the hang of it.

In school , that may be a teacher or classmate. At home it would be your PARENTS. At church it would be your Pastor, Sunday School teacher, etc.

The one Tutor you can always count on is The HOLY GHOST! That's what was missing from my life!

Jesus told us He was going away to prepare a place for us (heaven). But he knew that in the meantime we would still need guidance, comfort, and power to overcome all the things the devil uses to try to make us miss heaven. Jesus promised that the Holy Ghost would lead us into all TRUTH. But guess what, WE HAVE TO BE WILLING TO FOLLOW.

To make it to heaven YOU'VE GOT TO HAVE A MADE UP MIND!

The Holy Ghost is our Teacher, we are His students. Another word for *student* is *disciple*. Jesus said in order for us to be His disciples we must first DENY OURSELVES, TAKE UP OUR CROSS and FOLLOW HIM...DAILY!

Just like in school YOU HAVE TO WANT TO BE TAUGHT and be WILLING to OBEY. You've got to stay on top of your assignments if you really want to be successful.Don't just take my word for it. I'm sure you may know a few students who made the honor roll. Ask them how they made it. I'm sure they won't tell you it was by watching lots of TV, listening to garbage on the radio, and hanging out all night with their buddies. It was a SACRIFICE!

"Sacrifice? Aw, man! That sure doesn't sound like fun at all! It's not *that* serious!"

Oh, you don't think so? Remember the rich fool? He probably felt the same way. Look at what happened to him! His agenda was just to eat, drink and be merry. Just kick back and have FUN! But where is he now?

OBEDIENCE IS OFTEN A SACRIFICE!

The Bible says God calls us (the young) because we are strong, but He calls the old because they are WISE. They often have to remind us, the same roads we're going over, they've already been there! I didn't want to listen to the wisdom God provided for me through my parents and other adults. In fact, as far as I was concerned adults were considered ENEMIES.

Young person, that is a LIE from the pit of hell meant by the devil to keep us from following the counsel that could literally save our lives! A classmate once told me, "You gotta be careful. The people you think are your friends ain't always your friends". I found that to be true of my "enemies" too! Like the day my "mean, old, strict parents" arranged for me to be driven to school by another girl's mom.

All I had to do was walk a few blocks to her house and we could leave together. Instead, I left the house that morning, pretending to go the girl's house. But I had actually let a "friend" (BOYfriend to be exact) talk me into riding with him.

I found out who my true friends were. On my way to his house, I was snatched into an alley by a stranger and violated. When I returned to school, my "friends" all sat in a corner whispering- and laughing! One of them did ask if I was ok. My so called boyfriend laughed and said, "Sure she's ok. She's used to it." I had never been so humiliated in my life! Against the LOVING instructions of my parents- my true "friends" – I tried to please a true enemy!

The devil is the one that kept telling me I was missing all the fun and I would die lonely! But 1 John 4 says PERFECT LOVE CASTS OUT FEAR! That's what I needed! That's what I was searching for ...the PERFECT LOVE! And I found it when I accepted JESUS CHRIST!

DON'T MISUNDERSTAND! I am not at all suggesting that you can't ever have ANY true friends, real fun or really enjoy life if you choose to live your life for Christ. There is nothing wrong with eating, drinking or being merry! But some of us, like me and my "friends", took it to the extreme.

Some of us are suffering from the deadly virus BKS (BARBIE AND KEN SYNDROME)! Your whole life could be wasted away while you sit around waiting for and allowing somebody else to dress you, "play" with you or buy you a house!

Before I accepted Jesus Christ as my Savior and Lord, I was so confused! Confused about who to listen to. As a youth, I found myself listening to "friends" instead of parents and Godly role-models.

I wasted what could have been the best years of my life (my YOUTH) trying to be accepted by my "friends". Everything I wore, the places I went, the money I spent was all to please my 'friends". I wasted even more of my *adult* life in the church doing the same thing! Attending and participating in church programs because my "friends" were there. Giving extra money in the offering so my "friends" (and enemies) would see me "giving" and be impressed that I was "blessed".

And I don't know if I should even mention the many times I changed my "church-clothes" to please the well meaning "church-folks"! When I wore the long skirts someone said I looked too old and I should show my legs more! When I wore them shorter, someone else accused me of being "fast" and said I would make the "brothers" backslide! I got so fed up I decided to just do my own thing and not listen to NO-body. (I know that's terrible English but that's how irritated I was!) But that was not the will of GOD! I didn't understand that to truly be "accepted" I needed only to please God.

The Bible says:

"The way of a fool is right in his own eyes, but he that takes heed to counsel is wise".

(Proverbs 12:15- paraphrased).

But how can we know who to listen to when there are so many people giving us "conflicting" advice? When you hear two or three "good" ideas how do you know which one is really God's ideal for your personal life? Jesus said He came to give us LIFE and that more ABUNDANTLY! So He's the one you want to please!

In Psalm 37:4 it says if we delight ourselves in the Lord, He will give us the desires of our heart! *Delight* means to take GREAT PLEASURE in something or someone. It also means to give joy or satisfaction.

What satisfies God? Complete OBEDIENCE to HIS WORD. How can we understand what His Word wants us to do? By paying attention to and practicing what we are being taught by the teachers *He* provided for us. Parents, Pastors, Sunday School Teachers, even GOD-given friends!

Most importantly, we need to be filled with the HOLY GHOST! God's spirit dwelling in you will reveal to you who you should listen to, what to do, and when to do it!

By now you may be thinking, 'Okay. I hear what you're saying, But I still don't see how getting all involved in church and stuff is supposed to change my life." NO! Getting involved with "church and stuff" alone will *not* change your *life*.

Remember that a lot of the time I spent *working* in the church I was living in SIN! A FAITHFUL choir member! A NICE QUIET girl. The *change* came when I took the things I had been hearing and seeing in church and *applied* them *consistently* to my life. I had to get involved in a personal relationship with Jesus Christ!

Nobody could beat me handling my *church*-work, but I needed to learn to do my *home*-work too!

Praying daily – asking God to lead me strengthen me, protect me and help me please Him. (Matthew 6:13)

Studying God's Word - so I would know for myself what pleases Him and what doesn't. (2 Timothy 2:15)

Meditating on God's Word - whatever is on your mind will eventually show up in your words, actions and attitude.
(Psalm 119:11, Romans 12:1-2)

Obeying God- after finding out what He wants (and what He doesn't), allowing the Holy Ghost to give me power to say "no" to sin and to do the will of God.
(Romans 6:12-17)

Praising and worshipping God – expressing my gratitude to the Lord, privately and in the presence of others by my thoughts, words and deeds.
(Psalm 107:1-8, Psalm 19:14)

Witnessing – looking and preparing for opportunities to tell (and SHOW) others how the love of Christ can change them too! That's what I'm doing right now by sharing my story with you!
(Isaiah 43-:10)

I know living for God may seem impossible but YOU CAN DO IT! All it takes is a made up mind! The JOY of the Lord is your STRENGTH!

You know, I will never forget the day I accepted Christ and began my personal relationship with Him. It was kind of hard at first – going down to the altar, pregnant (again) in front of all my "friends" and all the other nice "church-folks" that thought I was just going to be away at school when I took my "leave of absence" from the choir. Somehow, however, the whispers and looks on their faces didn't even matter anymore once I took that first step.

No, it hasn't been all peaches and cream. No, it has not been easy. There have been lonely nights. There have been times I've had to go "without", in spite of unlimited opportunities to go "with". I was rejected by my "friends" in the world because I didn't party any more. I was even rejected by quite a few unforgiving "church folks" who felt I should be too ashamed of myself to even set foot in the place.

But JESUS is the only One that loved me, and HE LOVES YOU-UNCONDITIONALLY. In spite of all the wrong I've done, in spite of the material things I lost during my search for acceptance, He took me just as I was and made me what I am. And Jesus is willing and ready to do the same thing for you!

Am I perfect now?

NO WAY! But 1 Corinthians 5:17 says:

"If any man be in Christ he is a NEW creature; OLD THINGS HAVE PASSED AWAY and behold ALL THINGS ARE BECOME NEW!"

I tell people all the time now, "I'm not perfect, but I *AM* NEW!"

What's that? You say *your* life isn't all that bad? Okay. My response again is: REMEMBER THE RICH FOOL!!!

"COUNTING THE COST"

Now, I've told you my story. I told you how I was raised in church and loved every minute of it during my childhood, but got "bored" with it as I grew older. I told you how I believed the lies Satan told me through my "friends"- that I was missing all of the "fun ". I believed him. So, I went on out there to see what I was missing.

I won't lie. I did have some fun. But I paid a high price for it. Let's count up the cost, shall we?

It cost me my virginity.

Remember, the guy I lost it to didn't mind me going to church! He went with me! But he was really "nice" to me and gave me "nice" stuff. Even though I knew it was wrong, I felt "obligated". Imagine that! Feeling more obligated to a guy that gave me a few "nice" things vs. being obligated to The Man (Jesus) who gave Me His LIFE!

It cost me my reputation as a respectable young lady.

It wasn't even a few minutes before he had told all of our "friends" he had been with me! Not only that, hanging around with him also meant hanging with *his* friends. You know the old saying, "Birds of a feather flock together"? A lot of the things his friends were doing I wasn't even into. Nevertheless, I was labeled by our "friends", (excuse me), a "HOE!"

It cost me my job, financial stability and good credit rating.

Due to all the stress I was letting my "friends" take me through, and the mental torment from trying to live with one foot in the world and the other in church, I started performing poorly on the job – that is, when I managed to show up! Eventually I was re-hired, and thanks to my parents guidance I had A1 (excellent) credit for quite awhile-that is until I started trying to dress to impress my "friends".

I maxed out all 7 of my credit cards trying to shop with and sometimes shop *for* all my "friends". I even committed the ultimate no-no and co-signed for a "friend" to buy a car. I ended up paying the entire note myself! And along with the credit card bills, I still had a student loan to repay even though I never graduated. I held a full time job since 1987, but I wasn't able to afford my own car until 1994! And I'm still paying off some of those same credit cards! Remember! A CO-SIGNER IS NOTHING BUT A FOOL WITH A PEN!

It cost me my high school diploma *and* a college degree.

Remember? I got pregnant my sophomore year in high school and had to drop out. I did earn my GED and went on to college. But,remember? I dropped out because one of my "friends" kept steeling my bus fare and tuition so he could get high!

It cost me my relationship with my parents.

We were getting along great until I decided to start listening to my "friends", and the devil's lie that my parents were my enemies. They never stopped loving me, but they were finding it really hard to trust me. We couldn't even hold a casual conversation.

What hurt them the most is how I literally stood in their face, in front of my "friend" (which they kept trying to warn me was not really my friend) – and screamed to the top of my lungs, "YOU DON'T LOVE ME!" By the way, this is the same "friend" that tried to kill me with a baseball bat! I remember looking at my parents and thinking "I HATE YOU!" but I didn't get a chance to say anything else. See, Mom was saved, sanctified and filled with the Holy

Ghost, but my Daddy wasn't. Need I say more?

My "friend" just stood there and "let" my parents drag me off kicking and screaming. Ha! Some friend, right? I found out later Daddy had a loaded gun. My "friend" got us both in a lot of trouble, but my Daddy could have gone to jail and HE would have been dead!

It cost my children being raised without a father in an unstable home.
My son's father died of a heart attack. I was so irresponsible with my money, my kids spent most of their lives living with my parents, and occasionally my other "friends". I was so "out of it"; I was gone most of the time. My parents had to put me out twice; but despite my nasty attitude at the time, they never closed their doors to my kids.

It cost me my health.

I was constantly worn down physically from working full time (and overtime) to keep my bills paid and feed my kids. At the same time I was still trying to "do church". Many nights I'd fall asleep in the middle of a conversation, leaving them to put themselves to bed. I was worn out emotionally because I hardly ever had extra money for me, or my kids to have any "fun". And despite the fact I had changed some of my ways, I was always on a guilt trip because I knew my past financial folly was causing my whole family to suffer. Eventually I had a breakdown and had to take more time off work – unpaid.

It almost cost me my life.

Remember earlier I told you how my boyfriend tried to kill me? Not long after that, I almost succeeded in killing myself. I was driving alone by the lake one night, when suddenly I was just overwhelmed with guilt over all my past failures, and depression over my dark present. I couldn't even attempt to imagine a better future. I tried to see life getting better for us, but Satan had me convinced that a happy life just wasn't meant to be – at least not for me.

As I approached a concrete overpass a few miles ahead, I heard a cold slithery voice whisper in my ear, "Just let go of the wheel". I shuddered! NO WAY! My kids are already growing up without a father. I can't make them lose me too!"

Again that cold voice insisted, "Ha! They don't need you! You can't even afford to take care of them without your parents always having to help you! Go ahead! Let go! Your parents will take care of them!" I know it sounds crazy, but for a split second, that actually made sense! But I was SCARED! What if

I ran into somebody? It was one thing to kill myself but I didn't want some innocent bystander to get hurt! Hmm.

Funny how I wasn't thinking of my kids as "innocent bystanders! Nor my parents who would end up raising them! The "voice" was persistent, "Look around! It's after midnight. You're the only car on the road! Let go!" The overpass was now about 1/2 mile away. I gripped the wheel tighter and cried, "Oh God,no! It's not supposed to end like this! God help me!" The evil voice shouted it's final accusation, "YOU FAILED GOD! YOU ALREADY BLEW IT! NOW LET IT GO!!!"

A sick, dizzy sensation came over me. I can only tell you what happened as best as I can recall because everything seemed to be happening in a split second from that point on. I remember slumping over, and my forehead landing on the wheel as my hands drooped to my side.

I don't remember taking my foot off the accelerator, neither do I recall ever touching my brakes. All I remember after that is suddenly opening my eyes and seeing the front end of my car about to smash into the wall which was now right in front of me. Then suddenly, it felt like someone had snatched my hands and put them back on the wheel for me! At the same time I do remember screaming JESUS!- just in time to steer away from the wall!

As I straightened back into my lane, a white sports car whipped around me. Apparently it had approached from behind and saw me swerving so it sped on past. Once again, GOD MERCIFULLY and MIRACULOUSLY SPARED MY LIFE, as well as the other driver.

Now, remember how I thought getting back "into" church would make me happy? But I discovered that getting into church without getting into a relationship with Jesus Christ only added to my confusion and sense of loneliness. The Word of God I learned as a child was rooted deep in my heart. I knew too well what was right so it was hard to go back out in the world and try to live wrong. Yet I didn't feel like I "belonged" in the church because I still had a desire to do some of the "fun" things my "friends" in the world had taught me. So, I tried my best to live in both "worlds". But it just wasn't working! I was confused, lonely and SCARED! Do you want to know why?

"CHOICES"

46

In the twentieth chapter of the book of Exodus you will find the Ten Commandments. These are the basic laws God has given for His chosen people to live by in order to please Him. There are other instructions given throughout the entire Bible which are given in more detail, but they're all linked back to these ten original laws.

The very first commandment God gave to His chosen people says

"...*the Lord our God is one Lord. THOU SHALT HAVE NO OTHER GODS BEFORE ME*".

Not long after this commandment was given, the children of Israel whom God had delivered from slavery in Egypt, and chosen to be His people, went right back into the sin of idolatry – the worship of idol gods.

They were having all kinds of wild parties, overeating, getting drunk, and engaging in all kinds of immoral sex! And this wasn't just a one-time deal. No matter how often God worked miracles of protection and provision for them, they would "straighten up" only for a little while, then go right back to doing their own thing...with no shame!

These ungodly people were in a cycle of disobedience to God's laws. They constantly displayed their ingratitude in the presence of their ungodly neighbors. But God had chosen Israel to teach His laws (and KEEP them) so the other nations would learn to serve the Lord and be blessed.

Instead, their neighbors learned their wicked ways and their children were following in their footsteps! And each generation turned out to be even more wicked than their grandparents. Can you see why the world is in the condition it's in now?

When God gave us His laws, He was not trying to keep us from enjoying life! He gave His commandments so we could learn how to please Him. Then He promised if our ways please Him, He would bless us! The twenty-eigth chapter of Deuteronomy lists all of the blessings for being obedient to God.

We will be blessed when we rise up in the morning, and blessed when we lie down at night! We will lend and not borrow! We will be blessed when we go out and bless when we come in! Good health is even promised to those who obey. God said if we listen intently and diligently obey His laws, He would not allow any of the diseases that afflicted our enemies to afflict us! And He promised to bless our children...forever!

On the other hand, when God's laws are broken, pain, suffering and death always follow.

Romans 6:23 says,

"For the wages of sin is death, but the gift of God is eternal life through Jesus Christ our Lord"

So what happened? God's people knew what God commanded and He had proven to them over and over that He has the power to bless them. So why didn't they just do as He commanded and keep the laws? And why didn't they teach their children like He commanded them to? The children of Israel failed to obey God for the same reason I did.

FEAR OF REJECTION! They didn't want the other nations to laugh at the way they lived. They wanted God to bless them, and they knew they had to keep the law to be blessed. But they didn't want to lose their...

"F-R-I-E-N-D-S"! Wow! There's our favorite word again!

God told the children of Israel He would be their righteous king who would never enslave them like the Kings of Egypt had done. But as soon as He delivered them from bondage and brought them into their own land, they got together and decided "Hey! We want a king like all the other nations!"

God warned them through His prophet that if they put their trust in a human being to be their king, that king would overwork them and make them pay heavy taxes. He warned them that their sons would be forced to go to war and many more problems would arise. But they insisted, "We want to be like everyone else! Give us a king!"

Now God created every man with the right to choose between His Way – which is obeying His commandments and going his own way. No one has ever been forced to live for God. But no one has ever been forced to be blessed either! So God let them have a king (aka "president"). And sure enough, all that God said would happen to them is still going on to this very day, all over the world, isn't it?

The devil has tried to get us to accuse God of being unfair. He has many wondering if God really loves us, why does He allow such horrible things to go on in the world?

Well I can't answer that fully. No one can. However, God did promise to one day destroy this world because it *is* so full of wickedness.(Revelation 20). But the Bible tells us in 2 Peter 3:9

"...God is not willing that ANY should perish, but that all should come to repentance".

The same answer applies to the question "How could a loving God put people in hell?" GOD DOES NOT "PUT" NOR "SEND" PEOPLE TO HELL!

Again the Bible lets us know in 2Peter 2:4,9 that hell was created for Satan and His angels. So how is it that people end up in hell? Because God gave every man a choice. Choose His Son Jesus Christ as your Savior and Lord and allow Him to help you live pleasing to God and you will live forever with Him! **To choose NOT to live for God is to choose what Satan wants!**

Satan does not want you to live forever in heaven! He lost that opportunity himself when *he* got kicked out of heaven for CHOOSING not to obey GOD! (Revelation 12:7-9).That's right! Satan is so JEALOUS over the fact that you have the opportunity to take his place in heaven, that he's doing everything he can to keep you from getting there!

He knows the only way you can make it to heaven is by accepting Jesus Christ. He knows that Jesus will enable you by the power of the Holy Ghost to live your life pleasing to God. So he tries his best to get you to REJECT Jesus Christ!

Jesus said,

"I am the Way, the Truth and the Life. NO MAN COMES TO THE FATHER (GOD) except by ME!" (St. John 14:6)

So do you see how Satan turns this whole rejection thing around? He paints pictures in our minds so that we go through life believing it's more important to avoid being rejected by people, but when we go after their acceptance, we in turn end up rejecting CHRIST and the perfect will of GOD! And guess what? There is no "middle ground!"

The children of Israel wanted the best of both worlds. So they tried to keep God's commandments AND live like their ungodly neighbors. Guess what? It didn't work for them! And it won't work for us!

JESUS said, *"I am come the LIGHT of the world"*. (St.John 12:46) Those who don't have Christ are living in DARKNESS!

2 Corinthians 6:14 and Ephesians 5:11 remind us that *LIGHT HAS NO FELLOWSHIP (OR AGREEMENT) WITH DARKNESS!* When you're at home in your room, sometimes you want to turn a light on , and sometimes you want it off, right? Now what happens

when you go in your dark room and flip on the light? The darkness goes away, doesn't it? But you have never had the light on *and* off in your room at the same time have you?

Of course not! The same "rule" applies to the light of Christ that's to shine in us! When Christ returns to rescue us from God's final judgement and destruction of this world, only those who have His light in them will be saved! Jesus has warned us that no man knows the day nor hour He will appear! (Matthew 25:13, 24:42,44).

So let me ask those of you who want to keep playing around with your light switch: What if Jesus happens to return at the the split second you choose to flip your light *off?* You know, just for a "little" while to have a "little fun"?

The Bible says He will return in a moment, in the twinkling of an eye. (1

Corinthians15:52). Not the "blink" of an eye, but the "twinkle"! You've seen a person blink their eye before, but how many times have you actually caught the *twinkle* in someone's eye?

It happens so fast, you probably never have But again, because God IS too loving to just "put" people in hell, he gives EVERY man the opportunity to accept Christ for himself! And as for rejecting Christ, God's Word has made the consequences clear!

You know what else, God wants so much for us to choose His way but He also knows that because of Satan's tactics, the choice would not be easy and the time to make that choice won't always be available. So he sent His prophets to stir our minds to a decision.

He asked the people,

"How long will you be stuck between two opinions? If the Lord be God, serve Him!" (I Kings 18:21).

Another man of God urged the people:

"You choose this day who you will serve. If you choose God, you and your children shall LIVE!" (Deuteronomy 30:19 and Joshua 24:15).

Even Jesus Himself gave fair warning when He sent this message to one of His churches! (Revelation 3:15-22)

"I know your works...you are neither hot nor cold. I wish you would make up your mind and either be hot or cold! However, if you do not make a decision, I will spit you out!

We can't afford to try to "mix" with the world. There weren't many people that were bold enough to make that decision – to be "different" and not follow the ungodly ways of their ungodly worldy neighbors. Some tried to be "undercover" Christians and just not "bother" anyone.

But Jesus had two things to say to them:

"*You are the light of the world. A brightly lit city cannot be hidden, neither do men light candles and set them in the bushes.*" (Matthew 5:14-16)

"If you are ashamed (refuse)to own me before men, I will be ashamed (refuse)to own you before the Father!" (Matthew 10:33, Mark 8:38 and Luke 9:26).

THE CHOICE *IS* OURS!!!

"WHAT'S HAPPENING NOW"

The Bible says we overcome by the Blood of the Lamb [JESUS CHRIST] and by the word of our TESTIMONY! That's why I'm so glad you took the time to read this book! It's one of the *many* ways God is using me now to share the message of His love, grace and miracle working power!

Since I accepted Christ as my Savior and Lord, the Lord has restored broken relationships within my family. He has given me favor with my former employer who rehired and promoted me to a supervisory position, serving major clients in the marketing industry. I recently celebrated 15 years with the company! Am I saying my life is problem free since I've accepted Christ?

NOT AT ALL! In fact it's even tougher now because I've got an angry devil at my heels trying his best to destroy me. It's tougher now because the sinful things I enjoyed in the world now must be denied to walk with the Lord. That's not always easy. But my love for God has kept me. We maintain earthly relationships by doing what pleases the other person...IF WE VALUE THAT RELATIONSHIP. So it is in our relationship with the Lord. GREATER IS HE [JESUS] THAT IS IN ME THAN HE THAT IS IN THE WORLD! (1 John 4:4).

Now, who would have ever guessed that one day "little old me" would be writing books, plays, songs and traveling, reaching people with the Gospel of Jesus Christ! Well you know what? Had I kept looking at the negative circumstances I was in (mostly a result of my own bad choices and outright rebellion in my previous years), I know I wouldn't be alive right now to share my story with you.

You may be feeling *you* don't have much to offer anyone. You may be feeling *you* just have to settle for whatever life throws your way – that you don't *deserve* anything better.

Well guess what? YOU'RE RIGHT!

Without a personal relationship with Jesus Christ, none of us have anything, know anything nor can do anything OF OURSELVES that would make us good enough to make it into heaven, let alone help someone else along the way!

That's why Jesus Christ, the Son of the Living God came to earth and shed His Blood on the cross. He did it to pay for our sins so that we can be in relationship with God The Father and live forever with him! That's <u>PERFECT</u> LOVE! PERFECT LOVE CASTS OUT FEAR! (1 John 4:18)

Because of Jesus' willingness to be obedient to God the Father, even to the point of suffering and sacrificing His life for us, God raised Him from the dead and gave Him ALL POWER. That's right! JESUS CHRIST has TOTAL power over all works of the devil! And now Jesus want to share that love and power with YOU!

Dear young person, aren't you tired of hanging out with the wrong people, in the wrong places doing the wrong things? Hey, Church Girl, (or Church Boy)! Aren't you tired of pretending you've got it all together? Shouting on Sunday until your feet go to smokin' but not being able to say "no" to sex, partying, lying and gossiping through the week? Aren't you just fed up with trying to fit in?

Don't you wish you could just figure out where you really belong?

If this is your case, then you don't need to be accepted by a certain group of people. IT'S TIME FOR YOU TO ACCEPT JESUS CHRIST! It's time out for just looking for the right guy (or girl) to invite you out. IT'S TIME FOR YOU TO INVITE JESUS IN and let Him be your Savior, your Lord and that "BEST FRIEND" you've been longing for.

It's time out for "playing house" Saturday night and playing church Sunday morning! IT'S TIME FOR YOU TO GET REAL WITH JESUS! It's time for you to let Jesus fill that emptiness in your heart with TRUE LOVE. It's time to stop living in fear of getting "caught" or worse yet dying in your sin and going to hell!

It's time for you to let Jesus give you the victory over your sin and make you an effective witness for Him.

Aren't you ready to change?

IF YOU'RE <u>NOT</u> READY TO CHANGE:

It might interest you to know that I wasn't the only young person trying to live with one foot in the world and the other in church. But for some reason, out of thirteen fellow choir members that were playing the church game right along with me, I'm the only one left. Three died with AIDS, three died of other serious illnesses, three were murdered, and one was hit by a train. I'm not sure how the other two died. Nobody mentioned it so I didn't ask. I'm also not sure which of them , if any, gave their lives to Christ.

The last I saw them they were still eating, drinking and being merry. You know, just like the children of Israel. Oh, I didn't tell you what happened to the children of Israel did I? Well, Moses (their leader) told them whoever will serve the Lord, come and stand by me. The Bible doesn't say how many people moved, or how fast they got moving, but it does say that SUDDENLY there was an earthquake and where all those people that had not "stepped over" on the Lord's side were standing, the ground opened and swallowed them up! (Numbers 16:1-33).

Am I saying that's what happened to my friends? I can't say that because I don't know what they may have said to God before they drew their last breath. I would love to see all of them. But we won't know until...

Just please consider this. These were not young people that I had a chance to grow up *and* grow old with. They didn't just hit "thirty-something" and start dying off, either. They died *young*; and they all died within the space of less than three years. It was as if a judgment had fallen on my generation!

And let me also call to your attention that I didn't even count my other classmates and neighbors who died who were not in church at all.

These were CHOIR members mind you. Talented singers, directors and musicians. Am I telling you that all people in the church are playing games and living a "double" life? NO! But of a few hundred active members, we were thirteen that were!

Ironically, there were about 13 others that DID give their lives to Christ and now serving the Lord in ministry. I could have been numbered with either "half" of my generation. The choice was mine...the choice is YOURS!

If you're not ready to choose Christ and really live for Him, you might as well put this book down right now and go on back to whatever you were doing before. But don't waste your time "playing church!". Honestly. I mean why make matters worse on yourself? Why should you give all that money in the offering and pay choir dues if you're going to hell anyway? Might as well just eat, drink and be merry, now! You'll pay later!

But remember, God loved you so much, He made the way for you through His Son Jesus Christ. So you can actually choose between heaven and hell!

YES, THE CHOICE *IS* YOURS!

IF YOU ARE READY TO CHANGE:

PRAYER:

Lord Jesus, I am a sinner. I realize that no matter how nice of a person I may be, there is still nothing about me that qualifies me for heaven.

I am sorry for my sins, known and unknown; and starting today, this very moment ,I choose to turn from my sins and follow You!

I believe You are the Son of God. I believe You died on the cross to pay for my sin and rose again the third day to give me eternal life, because of your love for me.

Lord Jesus, I need YOU! I need Your love, Your grace to obey the things You require of me, and Your power to overcome the devices the devil will try to use against me. Lord Jesus I believe You will return again to take us to live with You forever. So, I am trusting You now to take control of my life, fill me with Your spirit, teach me Your way and prepare me for that Great Day! THANK YOU JESUS! AMEN!

Now, you will want to know more about how you can grow closer to God and keep the JOY of the LORD (which is your STRENGTH) flowing in your heart. So feel free to write us (or if possible stay in touch with the person who loved you enough to give you this book!) We're here to help you grow in your new relationship with the Lord!

"Remember NOW thy creator
IN THE DAYS OF THY YOUTH!"
Ecclesiastes 12:1.

"TO MY FAMILY"

These next pages are dedicated to my family. We have the power to choose the family we want to marry into. As adults, we can choose a child to adopt into our families. We can even choose to be Born Again into the family of God. What we do not have is the power to choose what family, the date or time we will be born into. Neither do we have the power to choose when we will die.

What we do have is the power to love, honor and if need be, forgive the families God saw fit to place us in, before we (or they) die. May these messages to my family stir you to consider how God can use you to bless your family. And know this, WITH GOD, ALL THINGS ARE POSSIBLE!

To My Son
"ED"

My First-Born, my Senior Bodyguard,
my "runnin' buddy"

Yeah, we both ran from the "church thing" for a long time. Thank God we got away and found out it's a JESUS THING!

Praise God for the Blood of Jesus that washes even us "black sheep" white as snow!

You've been a really patient illustrator and we've been through many "rough drafts" in life; but God has been faithful to both of us!

Thank you so much for just letting me be "Mom".

The seed of the righteous shall be delivered!

I LOVE YOU!

To My Son
"EMMANUEL"

When the doctors said you would never hear nor speak, I was devastated.

But little did we know God would use that experience to lay a foundation of faith for both of us. Every time I hear you play your own keyboard, drum and guitar compositions, I'm reminded of the night you uttered your first words in song: "Jesus Loves The Little Children" and recited your first Bible verse "with His stripes I am healed." (Isaiah 53:5)

Now, once again God has proven the devil to be a liar, and proven Himself to be the God that specializes in the IMPOSSIBLE!

Thank you for sharing your artistic talents in our first children's book, TOO MANY TOYS"..(I know, for a "small" fee of course!)

I LOVE YOU

To My Mom
"Bern"

You trained me in the way I should go; even though I strayed often, the Word you instilled in me was with me every where I went - whether I was in the right place or not. That same Word, watered and nurtured is sustaining me even now and has brought the increase in my natural and spiritual life.

It was the intention of the enemy to make us enemies. But because of Christ and the power of love and forgiveness we both found in Him, you and I have become Sisters, and the best of friends. No matter what I took you through, you refused to give up on me. You fasted and prayed, believing God's promise found in Isaiah 54, "All thy children shall be taught of the Lord, and great shall be their peace".

Thank you for everything, Mom! I LOVE YOU!

To My Daddy
Sammie Lee

Grandma always boasted that I could "talk good". But this is one time I can't find the words to express what you mean to me. Just like with Mom, the devil tried hard to make us enemies, but God's love and forgiveness working for and through us has made us the best of friends.

I'm sure back in the day when you and Mom said "I do", you had no idea what all you would have to do to keep us together. But we can all look where God has brought us from and know for certain, that when God placed you as the head of our family, He knew exactly what He was doing. God didn't make a mistake Daddy, and I hope you understand now, neither did you!

Thanks for always being there for me, even when I acted like I didn't want you to be. And no matter what my new name may be, I will always be "Sam's daughter". I LOVE YOU!

To My Brother
"Big Mike"

Okay! I did it! No let me rephrase that!
GOD DID IT!

We spent many a day in "the ring" together.

But even behind our worst fights, deep inside I always knew you were in my corner.

I've had very few real men in my life, and I wouldn't be alive or able to recognize a real man

if God hadn't placed you as my guardian angel.

Sibling rivalry almost made us enemies, but God's love made us the best of FRIENDS!

KEEP IT REAL, MAN OF GOD!!!

I LOVE YOU!!!

To My Sister
"Marcy"

Okay. Sister/ daughter / girlfriend/ psychiatrist / mentor. I'd have to write another book just to talk about the special relationship we have.

Jeopardy: A therapist would probably say we were co-dependent, dysfunctional and confused. "What is family?"
Ha! Ha! Ha!

You've grown into a beautiful wife, mother and woman of God. I think I'll name my next baby after you!

GOTCHA! You thought I meant a real live baby? No! I mean my next book:

"I THOUGHT I KNEW MYSELF"

(The story of Mikki and Marcy).
Stay sweet my Queen! "Issues" almost made us enemies, but God's love made us the best of FRIENDS!

I LOVE YOU!

To My Sister
"Tammy"

By man's definition you're my sister-in-law; but I'm radical so I call you my sister-in-grace and truth!

You were destined to be in this family – if for no more than to keep me sane!

Ha! Ha1Ha! Just kidding!

We both know your Divine Assignment and Appointment is even greater than that!

I know many times you ask yourself, "What have I gotten myself into?"

Would you believe me if I told you that you really didn't have a thing to do with it?

This ain't even about you!

(I know, I'm talking big and bad since my book is out, right? Ha! Ha! Ha!)

Girl, ain't no body mad but the devil!

IT'S ALL ABOUT JESUS!

You won my brother's heart: that almost made us enemies, but the love and plan of God made us the best of FRIENDS!!!

I LOVE YOU!

To My Brother
"Mac"

Mac, you won my sister's heart as your wife and mine as your sister and friend. A scripture in Proverbs says a friend is born for adversity. Mac, as you know I purposely had no male friends in my life for a very long time. But God knew that every once in awhile, I needed to hear what a man had to say about certain situations – even if I didn't always agree.

I learned so much from you about life, love, commitment and responsibility. But most of all I learned about true friendship. A true friend can fall out with you and still be your friend. A true friend can take you at your worst, wait it out, pray it out and cry it out with you while God transforms you into His best.

You've been there for me through it all, Mac and I appreciate you for that. The generation gap (and a few other "issues") almost made us enemies; but God's love, forgiveness and Divine Appointment made us the best of FRIENDS!

I LOVE YOU!

To My Auntie
"Ann"

By blood you're my aunt. But by God's design, you were my big sister. In spite of all the challenges we both faced growing up, you always found a way to have fun and make me laugh. It was so hard letting you go when you grew up and got married. I felt so abandoned. But every laugh we shared keeps me laughing to this day. And knowing that for all your trouble God has restored to you double and wiped your tears away, I rejoice for you!

You are so special, and I'm glad the Lord made you my Aunt, my Sister and my FRIEND!

Ann, the worst is truly over! The best is yet to come! Just walk into your season!

I LOVE YOU!

P.S. Oh yeah! I knew there was something else I needed to thank you for. Girlfriend, if it wasn't for you, I would have never known the miracle of hair-weave! THANK YOU, THANK YOU! THANK YOU!!! (smile)

To My Grandma
"MamaCis"

Grandma, I always loved your warm smiles and quiet ways. I couldn't wait to come to your house after school each day and sit with you by the window. I was very young then and to be honest I don't remember very much of what you said. I just remember feeling very loved, very happy and laughing a lot.

What I love most about you even now is how you never pretend to know everything. But what you do know, you pretend you don't know so we learned how to think for ourselves. You're a wise woman. I hope all of us grand and great-grandkids realize the treasure God gave us when He gave us you!

Thank you for everything!
I LOVE YOU!

In Loving Memory of My Grandpa "Daddy Frank"

"Daddy Frank" was somebody special.
I'll tell you the reason why.
He had a strange way of making you laugh even after he made you cry. He came across as a mean man. Not big on hugs and a kiss. He was a firm believer until the day he passed on, a man should have his wish.

I know it wasn't all peaches and cream.
And there still may be many regrets.
But if "Daddy Frank" could come talk to us now, he'd say you'd best forgive and forget.

Oh how I wish "Daddy Frank" was here now to see where God has brought us from!

But I'm glad I did get to tell Granpa that I love him from my heart.

I STILL LOVE YOU, GRANPA!
ALL IS WELL

To My Entire Family

I want to thank all of you: aunts, uncles, cousins far and near for the impact you have had on my life. The good and the bad, God used it all to make me into the woman I am today. There is a saying that there is a "black sheep" in every family. But I (and you) are a LIVING TESTIMONY that though our sins may be red as scarlet and our hearts black as midnight, the Blood of Jesus washes white as snow! So don't give up on our little lost/black sheep! But let's PRAY for them that they find their way to the Good Shepherd of their souls! THANK YOU! I LOVE YOU ALL!

" TO MY FRIENDS"

God has instilled in each of us gifts and talents to bless others, and to sustain ourselves financially. These pages are dedicated to people God chose as my friends. I say God chose them because each one came into my life by God's Divine plan.

They are not people I would have chosen for friendship because on the surface, we had little or nothing in common.

But as we sought to please God, HE strategically ordered our steps, caused our paths to meet and we've been serving the Lord and each other ever since.

Each one has her or his own testimony of past and present struggles. But not one of them was so preoccupied with their personal "issues" – or successes-that they couldn't take time out to touch the lives or meet the needs of others. The Blood of Jesus made us family, the love of Jesus made us the best of FRIENDS!

My Friend
"Jackie"

About 10 years ago I met "Jackie".
It was a friendship ordained by God.
I know it was a divine set up from Him,
for to me she seemed a bit odd.
See she wasn't like
so- called friends from my past
who only liked me for what I could give.
But when I was broken and wanted to die
she stuck by me and commanded me,
" LIVE"!
When others were busy tearing me down
and ripping my heart at the seam,
God often used Jackie to pick me up
and rebuild my self-esteem.
Jackie admits, "I'm not perfect"!
And I quickly say "Neither am I".
But God has used us in each other's lives
to make us both more like Christ.
Here's how you can know if the friends you're
with are sent from God above .
When you have nothing material to offer
and they still shower you with LOVE.
Through our good times and through the bad

Jackie and I came to discover
that JESUS IS OUR <u>VERY</u> BEST FRIEND!
Yes, He's closer than any brother.

To My Friend
"Laresha"

You were my youth choir president, then my
friend.
For a season, I became your enemy,
Yet you remained my friend.
You were my boss, and still my friend.
Now I am your Sister in Christ, and your
friend.
I suppose the saying is true:
Through All Of Life's Changes
We'll Always Be Friends.

Looking for a "Daycare" Staff? - (smile)
I LOVE YOU!

My Friend
"Carla"

Hmm...there's so much to say about Carla.
This woman is one of a kind.
She invited me home for dinner one day,
and fed my body and mind.
Her good old down-home cooking,
warmed me to the bone.
But what was even more satisfying
was the dessert she served my soul!
She encouraged me with the Word of God
And a bit of her testimony.
Then Carla turned and told me to pray,
I thought to myself "who me?"
Again she picked up my spirit,
filled with low self-esteem and doubt.
Again she reminded me Whose I am,
And just 'cause I'm down, I ain't out!
So together we prayed and sang praises,
Like Paul and Silas in jail.
And enjoyed the presence of our Awesome God
Who can do anything but fail!
I'm so grateful that God chose Carla
to be a part of my life.
For her life is a living example of how
God will make everything alright!

"DEDICATIONS"

Special Dedication and Thanks
To Apostle Richard D. Henton

Dear Pastor Henton,

Thank you so much for sharing with us your testimonies of God's faithfulness to you during your service to Him as a young minister. The testimony/message that impacted me most was "Don't Wreck The Train!"

Thank you for not wrecking that train! For I was one of millions that needed a ride! Thank you for the many open doors and thank you for encouraging me to walk on in and "TAKE IT". I LOVE YOU!

Special Dedication and Thanks
To Evangelist Carolyn D. Henton

Dear First Lady Henton,

You know, you could have been content to just be "Lady Di"; just an elegant showpiece to add a touch of softness and class, to decorate the pulpit. Instead, you allowed the Lord to prepare you and place you in the Kingdom for such a time as this. And like Queen Esther, you were not afraid to press beyond the realm of traditions to save an entire nation. I just can't find the words to express how thankful I am for your sacrifices. I can only pray and look forward to God enabling me to do the same! Stay beautiful! I LOVE YOU!

To
"Mamacita" Chestang

Mamacita,
You have been to me what the Apostle
Paul was to young Timothy,
A mentor and a friend.
Paul told Timothy
"Do not neglect the gift that is in you;
stir it up!"
It was in Children's Church Ministry
that the Lord blessed me to discover
and build the confidence to use the
talents He invested in me for his glory.
I thank you for your patience,
friendship, correction, guidance,
encouragement and love.
You're one of a kind!

To Aunt "Reen"

When I sit down and count all of
Grandma Fannie's sisters, you're always
on the list!
As a little girl, I looked forward to
coming to your house even when
"LeeLee" wasn't there to play with me.
I know you didn't always feel like
laughing. But even when you were upset,
you still had a built-in smile.
There's a tone of joy in your voice, even
in times of testing and sorrow.
Yes, Auntie Reen I must say
that from you I learned
THE JOY OF THE LORD IS OUR
STRENGHT!

To The Loving Memory of
My Grandaddy
"Willie"

Not knowing how "Tang" and "Kool-Aid"
really "worked", I watched in amazement
as my Grandaddy stirred plain old water
in a peanut butter or mayonnaise jar
with a spoon, and made it turn orange
(or purple).
"Oooh, Grandaddy! What's that?"
"Aw this? It's somethin' to drink!"
"Gulp...smack...yummm! Oooh! Grandaddy!
This is GOOD somethin' to drink!"

Well, now I'm a "big girl". I'm still
amazed at all the simple things my
Grandaddy made so special.
It's those simple things that are now
the treasures of my heart.

To The Loving Memory of
My Grandmama
"Fannie Mae"

Grandma Fannie was always excited
Over the things God gifted me to do.
Writing poetry and plays...
I can sing a little too!
My first book was completed
Before Grandmama passed away.
"You know my granddaughter's an author'
I remember hearing her say.
I keep pens and paper always on hand,
and here's the reason why,
Grandmama's parting words to me were
"Baby, don't let it die!"

To The Loving Memory
Of my Godmother
Mary Brooks-Wilson

I can't believe Mama Mary's not here to share this
special time with us.
But the special faith-seed she planted in my heart when
I was a little girl suffering with asthma is the
everlasting essence of my life.
I remember crying on her lap as she braided my hair. I
asked her
"Godmama, why do I have asthma?" I was about 8 years
old. Tears tied under my chin as I watched my cousins
running, laughing and playing,
Seemingly without a care in the world.
"Baby, I don't know", she said in her consistently
soothing voice,
"But don't worry, when you get big you won't have it
anymore."
About three years later, a woman named Evangelist
Meriweather came to my Grandmother's church. She put
her hand on my chest and prayed,
"I command your lungs to be opened in the name of
JESUS".
I've been asthma-free, needing no more allergy shots,
oxygen or medication ever since.

Let Everything That Has <u>Breath</u>
PRAISE THE LORD!!!

To
Strength In Unity Ministries:

Elder Robert and Freddie Childress
Don and Toby Robinson
Minister Ralph E. Mercer

My Dear Friends,

Galatians 6:1 says "Brethren, if a man be
overtaken in a fault, ye that are spiritual
restore such a one in the spirit of meekness;
considering yourselves lest ye also be
tempted".

I don't know where I would be if I didn't have
you in my corner during my process of spiritual
restoration and recovery.   There was never a
favor to great for me to ask of you.

With the Word of God as the foundation for
our relation-ship, we have transcended and
overcome every barrier the enemy tries to set
up to divide the Body of Christ; age, gender
and doctrinal differences.   Thus, the vision and

mission of Strength In Unity Ministries has manifested.

Let us continue to be steadfast, unmoveable and always abounding in the work of the Lord, for we know our labor in the Lord is not in vain.

THANKS FOR EVERYTHING! I LOVE YOU ALL!!!

And the "LAST" shall be "FIRST"

Dear Jesus,
We have a saying down here,
"Saving the Best for Last"
But You said something Yourself even more
profound and befitting:
The Last shall be FIRST"
I don't know why it took all this time for me
to realize that You are my Best Friend.
I don't know why I spent my whole life
searching for true love when You ARE love!
You are Alpha and Omega which means You
are the Beginning and the End;
the First AND the Last.
Thank You for Your mercy and patience
toward me as I found my way back to You,
My FIRST (and LAST)
LOVE!

MY SEARCH FOR ACCEPTANCE
("Epilogue")

I heard this song of worship to the Lord by "Israel & New Breed" just a few weeks before this book was to be released.

You've won my affection!
You've captured my heart!
You've won my devotion;
My worship is Yours!
You've won my affection!
You've captured my heart!
You've won my devotion;
Now I am Yours,
Completely Yours, forever!
I see the sacrifice You made;
I see the awesome price You freely paid!
You went the distance! You finished strong!
We were Your passion so You gave Your all!
Now, I am Yours
Completely Yours forever!

"CREDITS"

"Now there are diversities of gifts, but the same Spirit".

1 Corinthians 12:4

A few years ago, I heard a song by the Christian artists Kurt Carr & The Kurt Carr Singers called "No One Else".
The song says:

*Every man must use the gift he's given,
and every man must do the will of God.
You were created for a reason and chosen for a season.
So never feel your gift is just too small.
Never feel like what you have is least of all.*

*No one God created is just like you.
No one on the earth is quite the same.
In the Body of Christ there's a need for your life.
There's a purpose and assignment just for you.
There's a purpose for the gift that lies in you!*

*No one else can preach your sermon,
No one else can sing your song,
No one else could ever do what God has chosen you to do.*

Your gift was given from above
A blessing from the Father's love
So use your gift to the glory of God.

God created you with something inside that could not only change but literally save someone's life. How many doctors and nurses started out putting bandages on their dolls and checking their teddy bear's pulse?

What is your gift? What is your passion? What is God's purpose and assignment for you?

"...I long to see you that I may impart unto you some spiritual gift to the end that you may be established."

Romans 1: 11

God puts people in our lives to help us discover and perfect the gifts that He placed in us. These God-given tutors and mentors will not only encourage us to develop our talents but also help build in us Christ-like character so that we can handle the successes (and disappointments) that come along with grace. These have been my tutors:

Dr. W. Vance Washington (aka "Elder Dad") - Sunday School Teacher and President of the Board of Elders at Monument of Faith Church. Elder Dad helped me realize that Sunday School isn't just for kids. He instilled in me the passion to stand on the principles in the Word of God. Favorite quote: 'Let _God_ be God.'

Evangelist Shirley Green and Brother Larry Robinson –
During my childhood and preteens my Mother (an accomplished pianist) taught me "music basics". She and I sang duets together and I

served as an assistant choir directress in 3 churches throughout my life.

Evangelist Green and Brother Larry encouraged the "resurrection" of my passion for music that I lost during the turmoil of my journey back to God. Comparing myself to other "good" singers I thought "I can't sing".

They are both effective ministers of music in demand.

Under their tutelage I've drawn the conclusion that the only person who can not sing is one who won't open their mouth.

Pastors Pete and Constance Randall –
Took me under their wings and demonstrated to me what it really means to serve the Lord and others with the whole heart. Favorite quote: *'Lord, possess the part of me that you have need of'.*

Hats off to the following friends, families, businesses and ministries who offered their resources to help make this production possible. Only God could ever pay what you're really worth!

FRONT COVER DESIGN
Fernando Family Studio (Anita's photo) ,
Alvin James (Editor for Anita's photo),
Shirleen Evans (Anita's Braids),
Debra Hampton (Anita's costume) and the
The 1st Books Cover Design Team

BACK COVER DESIGN
John Cox - (Family portrait)
1st Books Cover Design Team

ILLUSTRATIONS
Emmanuel Hoover

PUBLIC RELATIONS AND DISTRIBUTION
My Parents, Sam & Bernice Hoover
Willa Mae Pullins and Evangelist Georgia Ford

CONTRIBUTIONS AND PRAYER SUPPORT
- Edward Hoover
- Elder Robert and Minister Freddie Childress, Ministers L. Don and Toby Robinson and Minister Ralph E. Mercer of Strength In Unity Ministries

116

- Pastor David Bates & Family of the Chapel at Olive Branch Mission - Chicago
- Bishop Bennie Allison and Corinthian Temple Church of God in Christ
- Pastor Woodard Williams and New Mt. Sinai Missionary Baptist Church
- My Pastor, Apostle Richard D. Henton and Family at Monument of Faith Church

And Especially Evangelist Mary Smith-Hampton, author of
"Child Bride" for introducing me to 1st Books Library!

About the Author:

Anita now lives with her sons in Chicago, IL and is currently serving as a Sunday School teacher and licensed minister, at *Monument of Faith Evangelistic Church* under the leadership of *Apostle Richard Daniel Henton.* Through her years of experience and walking with the Lord was birthed DOTYM (Days of Thy Youth Ministries), a vehicle by which she and her family have produced and distributed this and many other creative tools for sharing the Gospel of Jesus Christ.

DOTYM / Days of Thy Youth Ministries
P.O. Box 44188
Chicago, IL 60644